Animal Riddles

Einstein Sisters

KidsWorld

Q: What kind of key opens a banana?
A: A monkey.

Spider monkeys live in groups called "troops." When troops meet, the monkeys hug each other.

Spider monkeys use their long arms and tails to swing from branch to branch and tree to tree. They hardly ever come down to the ground.

Spider Monkey

Honey Bee

A honey bee's **wings beat** about **200 times per second.** The **wingbeats** make the bee's **buzzing sound.**

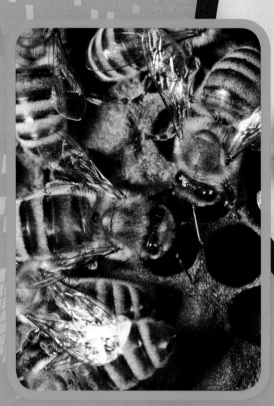

It takes almost **600 honey bees** to make **half a kilogram** of honey. They have to collect **nectar** from about **2 million flowers.**

Q: What letter can hurt you if you get too close?
A: B (bee).

Q: What is the difference between a crazy rabbit and a counterfeit bank note?
A: One is a mad bunny and the other is bad money!

Eastern Cottontail

More than half the world's rabbits live in North America.

Eastern cottontails are a kind of rabbit. They are named for their **white,** fluffy tails.

Whooping Crane

Whooping cranes are the **tallest birds** in **North America**. **They are about 1.5 metres tall.** They **live near** **marshes** and **lakes**.

Whooping cranes **nearly disappeared.** In 1941, there were **only 16 birds.** Today, there are **about 600.**

Q: What kind of bird can carry the most weight?
A: A crane.

To **make a nest,** barn swallows collect small balls of mud in their beaks. They **mix the mud** with **grass** and stick the balls together.

Barn swallows spend **most** of their time **flying**. They catch insects and even drink while in flight.

Q: What bird is with you at every meal?
A: A swallow.

Barn Swallow

Lion

Q: Why do lions
eat raw meat?
A: Because they
can't cook.

The **lion** is the second largest cat in the world. Lions only **live** in Africa.

Only **male** lions have **manes.** The **oldest lions** have the **darkest manes.**

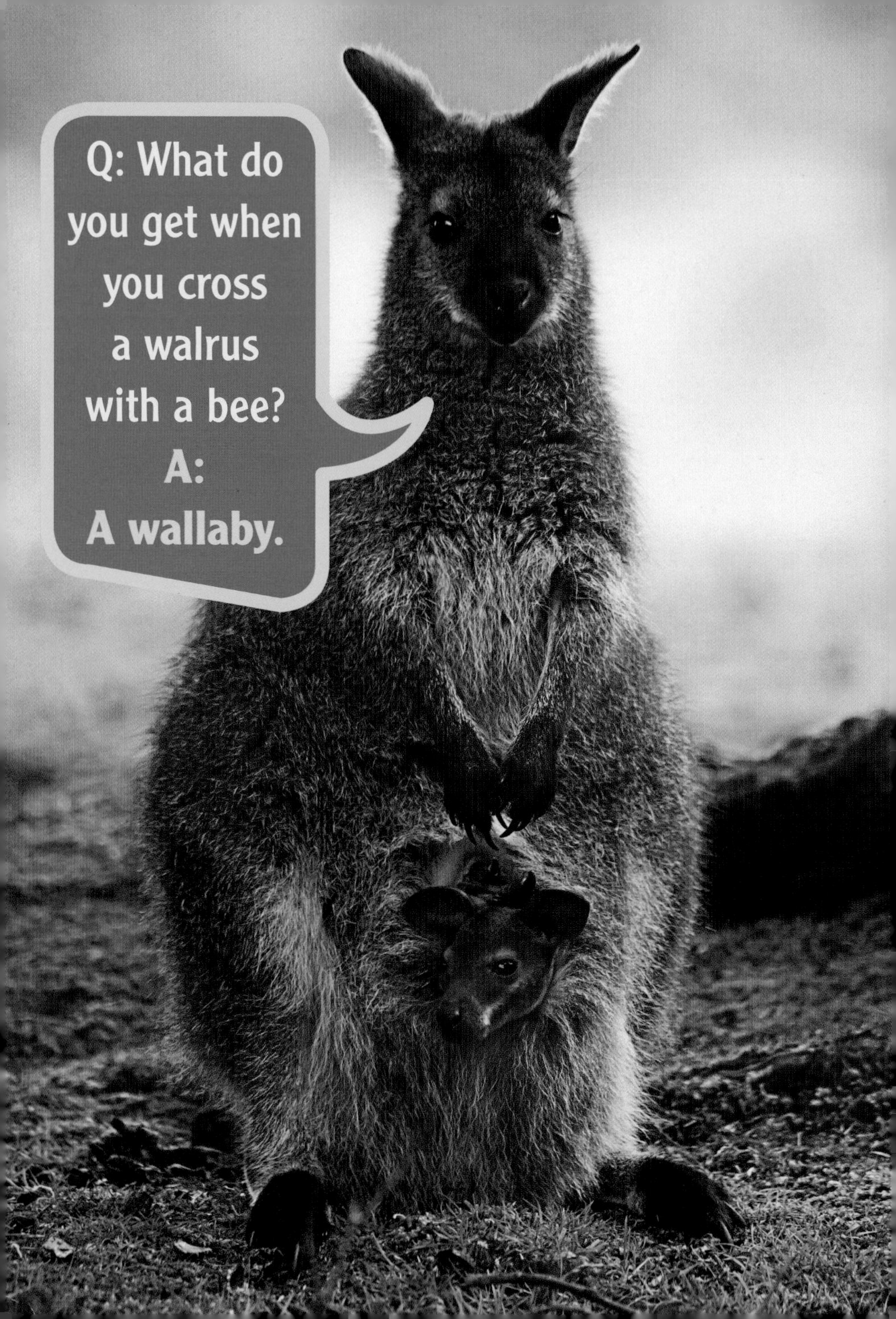
Q: What do you get when you cross a walrus with a bee?
A:
A wallaby.

Wallabies are
related to kangaroos,
but they are smaller.
They also have pouches
that they use to
carry their young.

Wallaby

Wallabies come from Australia.
There are more than
30 kinds of wallabies.

Sea Star

Starfish are also called "sea stars." They aren't fish. They are **related to sea urchins** and **sand dollars.**

Q: What fish only swims at night?
A: A starfish.

Most sea stars **have five arms.** Some have **10, 20** or even **40** arms. If a sea star **loses an arm**, it **grows a new one.**

Q: If you see a swimmer being chased by 12 sharks, what time is it?
A: Twelve after one.

The shark's **smooth torpedo shape** helps it **move quickly** through the water. Its shape **inspired the design** of the submarine.

The **great white shark** is named for its white belly. Most sharks are **dark on top** and **pale underneath**.

Great white shark

Kangaroo

Kangaroos have big, strong tails. The **kangaroo's** tail **helps it balance** and turn **when it hops.**

Kangaroos can't walk, they can **only jump. They can't jump** backwards.

Q: What jumps when it walks and sits when it stands?
A: A kangaroo.

Galapagos Tortoise

Galapagos tortoises often live more than **100 years**. They are the **longest lived** of all **land animals**.

Q: Where did the tortoise get a new shell?
A: From the hard-wear store.

When male Galapagos tortoises **"fight,"** they face each other and **stretch** their necks as **high** as possible. The **tortoise** with the **longest neck** wins the fight.

Polar Bear

Q: What's white, furry and has wheels on its paws?

A: A roller bear!

A polar bear's **fur** is **not really white.**
The **hairs** are **clear and hollow**
like **tiny straws.**

Polar bears are
the **biggest** bears.
They only live in
the Arctic. They
mostly eat seals.

The name **centipede** means "100 feet," but centipedes can have from **20** to **300 feet.**

Q: What is on the ground and a hundred feet in the air?
A:
A centipede on its back.

There are about **8000** different kinds of centipedes. They live all over the world.

Centipede

Porcupine

A porcupine's **soft hair** is mixed with **sharp quills.** It has about **30,000 quills.**

Q: What pine has the longest needles?
A: **A porcupine.**

Porcupines like to climb trees. They eat leaves, twigs and bark. They love salt.

Q: Who comes to a picnic but is never invited?
A: Ants.

Carpenter Ant

Carpenter ants **don't eat wood.** They **chew it** to make **nest cavities** and **tunnels.**

There are more than **1000 kinds** of carpenter ants. The **biggest** carpenter ants are nearly **1 centimetre** long.

African Penguin

African penguins **live** along the coast of southern Africa. **Most** other penguins live in **Antarctica**.

Q: Which side of a penguin has the most feathers?
A: The outside.

These **penguins** dive underwater to catch fish, squid and shellfish. An African penguin can **hold its breath** for more than 2 minutes.

Q: What grows up while growing down?

"Down" is a layer of fine feathers under the goose's outside feathers. The down keeps the goose warm.

A: A goose.

Canada geese usually **live near water.** You often see them in **fields** and **parks**, but they also **visit airports** and golf courses.

Canada Goose

A **mallard** is a kind of duck.
The **male** mallard has a
shiny, green head.
The **female is brown.**

Mallard

Duck feathers have an oily coating that makes them waterproof.

Q: When a duck has no money, what does it tell the waiter?
A: Put it on my bill.

Flying foxes eat **fruit**, **flowers** and nectar. They use **smell** and **eyesight** to find food.

Q: What animal is the best at baseball?
A: A bat.

Flying Fox

Flying foxes are large bats. The name "fox" refers to their reddish hair. They are some of the biggest bats in the world. They live in East Africa, Southeast Asia and Australia.

Garden Snail

The garden snail's **muscular foot** produces **mucus**. The mucus lets the snail **glide over** rough surfaces.

Snails are famous for **moving slowly.** The garden snail's fastest speed is **1.3 centimetres per second.**

Q: What is the strongest animal?
A: A snail—it carries its house on its back.

The elephant is the **biggest land animal** in the world. It is the **only animal that** can't jump.

Q: What is as big as an elephant but weighs nothing?
A: The elephant's shadow.

Elephant

Elephants only have four teeth. Each tooth is about the size of a brick.

Giant Panda

Pandas like to sit on the ground and eat, but they are good tree climbers, too. They also swim well.

Giant pandas are found in the mountains in China. They only eat the leaves and shoots of bamboo.

Q: What's black and white, black and white, and black and white?
A: A panda bear rolling down a hill.

Bluefin Tuna

Bluefin tuna are **warm-blooded**, like **humans**. They are **comfortable swimming** in the **cold** waters of the **North Atlantic**. Most fish are **cold-blooded**.

The **shiny bluefin tuna** is about **2 metres long.** That's **longer** than an **adult human** is **tall.**

Q: What's the difference between a fish and a piano?

A: You can tune a piano, but you can't tuna fish.

Rhinoceros means
"nose horn." The horn
is made of keratin.
Your fingernails and hair
are also made of keratin.

Rhinoceros

The **rhinoceros** is the **second-largest** **land animal**. The **elephant** is the **largest**.

Q: What has a horn but doesn't honk?
A: A rhinoceros.

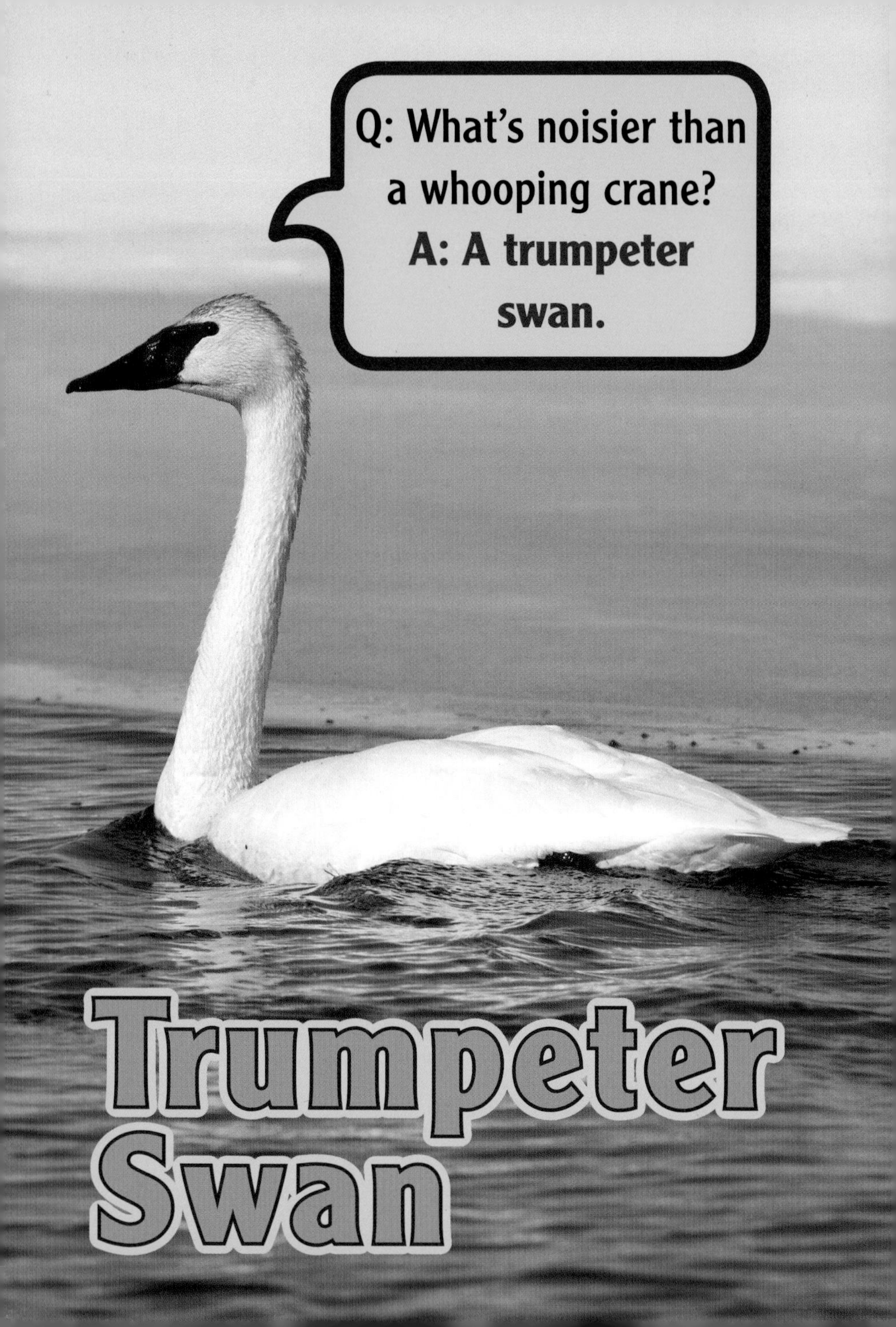

Trumpeter Swan

The trumpeter swan is the **largest** and **heaviest** waterbird in North America. It can weigh 13 kilograms. That's about as much as a **toddler**.

This **swan** is named for its loud, **bugle-like call.**

Emerald Tree Boa

Emerald tree boas **live** in **South America.** They **grow** to be as **long** as an adult is tall.

Q: What do you get when you cross a snake with a construction site? A: A boa constructor.

The emerald tree boa is a kind of constrictor. It catches prey with its teeth, then squeezes it to death and swallows it whole. It eats mostly birds and small mammals such as rats.

Q: What is the difference between a car and a buffalo? A: A car only has one horn.

The African buffalo is also called "Cape buffalo." It is **very dangerous.** A buffalo can even **kill** a **lion** or a **hyena.**

Male buffalo have bigger horns than the females. The horns grow together in a "boss" in the middle of the buffalo's head.

African Buffalo

Coyote

Coyotes often live in family groups called packs. Sometimes many coyotes will yip and "sing" together in a chorus.

The coyote is a member of the dog family. It lives almost everywhere in Canada, even in cities.

Q: What's the difference between a coyote and a flea?
A: One howls on the prairie and the other prowls on the hairy.

Most salmon are born in freshwater rivers and lakes. After they hatch, they **swim to the ocean.** They return to the **place** where they **were born** to reproduce.

Salmon

Baby salmon
are called
"fry."

Q: What part
of a fish weighs
the most?
A: The scales.

The scarlet macaw is a **kind of parrot.** It lives in the **tropical** parts of **South America.** You can also see it **in zoos.**

Q: A monkey, a squirrel and a parrot are racing to the top of a coconut tree. Which one will get the banana first?

A: None of them. Bananas don't grow on coconut trees!
This bird usually lives for 40 or 50 years, but some scarlet macaws live for more than 70 years.
Scarlet Macaw

Q: What kind of fish goes well with peanut butter?
A: Jellyfish.

Jellyfish **don't** have a brain. **They have a** network **of nerves** in their **skin** called a "nerve net."

There are many kinds of jellyfish. Some are **smaller** than a **pinhead**. Other jellyfish are **bigger** than **a human**. Not all jellyfish have **tentacles.**

jellyfish

The Publisher: KidsWorld Books

Library and Archives Canada Cataloguing in Publication

Animal riddles / Einstein Sisters.

ISBN 978-0-9940069-6-7 (pbk.)

1. Animals—Juvenile humor. 2. Riddles, Juvenile. 3. Wit and humor, Juvenile. I. Einstein Sisters, author

PS8375.A55 2015   jC818'.602   C2015-901521-9

Cover Images: Front cover: scarlet macaw, czecma13/Thinkstock. *Back cover:* lion, ecoimages-photos/Thinkstock; honey bee, IMNATURE/Thinkstock.

Background Graphics: abstract background, Maryna Borysevych/Thinkstock, 7, 19, 31, 43, 55; abstract swirl, hakkiarslan/Thinkstock, 13, 25, 49; pixels, Misko Kordic/Thinkstock, 3, 4, 5, 8, 10, 11, 15, 16, 17, 20, 22, 23, 26, 28, 29, 32, 34, 35, 39, 40, 41, 44, 47, 51, 52, 53, 56, 58, 59, 63.

Photo Credits: From Flickr: bobistraveling, 9; Kristin Shoemaker, 6–7; Matthew Hunt, 6; nature80020, 34–35; Tambako The Jaguar, 38. *From Thinkstock:* abadonian, 40; Anup Shah, 3, 13; BigRedCurlyGuy, 22–23; Byrdyak, 54–55; c-foto, 48–49; CarolinaBirdman, 10–11; craighind, 32; czardases, 27; czecma13, 60–61; DanBachKristnesen, 58–59; ecoimagesphotos, 12–13; EcoPic, 33; felin2, 41; frederic prochasson, 62; Fuse, 22, 45, 59; Geoff Kuchera, 56; guidemark50, 39; Harry-Eggens, 19; Henrik_L, 28, 29; Hung_Chung_Chih, 44; IMNATURE, 4–5; IPGGutenbergUKLtd, 15; Jameson Weston, 8; John Carnemolla, 20; JohnPitcher, 24–25; Juha Remes, 36; Jupiterimages, 28; kitiara65, 16; klauspeters, 51; LUNAMARINA, 46–47; Matthew Antonino, 42–43; Meike Marks, 21; MikeLane45, 2; Mirko_Rosenau, 36–37; nenadpress, 10; Purestock, 28–29; reptiles4all, 26; Richard Rodvold, 57; sergeyskleznev, 52; SteveOehlenschlager, 50; tae208, 16–17; Tony_Herbert, 14; vladoskan, 18–19; ZambeziShark, 43; Zoonar RF, 4; zysman, 52–53.

We acknowledge the financial support of the Government of Canada through the Canada Book Fund (CBF) for our publishing activities.

 Canadian   Patrimoine
Heritage   canadien

PC: 30